The Hangry Dictionary Definition Create Your Own Cookbook

A Penelope Pewter Production

han·gry

/ˈhaNGgrē/ · *adj*

The state of anger induced by the lack of food;

An increasingly negative emotional state

triggered by declining blood sugar levels.

Blank Recipe Journal

www.InspirationalWares.com

Recipes

Recipe:

Ingredients:

❖ _____ ❖ _____

❖ _____ ❖ _____

❖ _____ ❖ _____

❖ _____ ❖ _____

❖ _____ ❖ _____

❖ _____ ❖ _____

❖ _____ ❖ _____

Category:
❑ Appetizer
❑ Beverage
❑ Sauce
❑ Soup
❑ Entrée
❑ Dessert

Type:
❑ Fish
❑ Meat
❑ Poultry
❑ Vegetables
❑ N/A

Prep Time:

Cook Time:

Servings:

Directions:

_____

_____

_____

_____

_____

_____

_____

_____

_____

Rating: ☆ ☆ ☆ ☆ ☆

Notes & Comments:

Recipe:

Ingredients:

❖ _____

❖ _____

❖ _____

❖ _____

❖ _____

❖ _____

❖ _____

❖ _____

❖ _____

❖ _____

❖ _____

❖ _____

❖ _____

❖ _____

Category:
❑ Appetizer
❑ Beverage
❑ Sauce
❑ Soup
❑ Entrée
❑ Dessert

Type:
❑ Fish
❑ Meat
❑ Poultry
❑ Vegetables
❑ N/A

Prep Time:

Cook Time:

Servings:

Directions:

_____

_____

_____

_____

_____

_____

_____

_____

_____

_____

Rating: ☆ ☆ ☆ ☆ ☆

Notes & Comments:

Recipe:

Ingredients:

❖ _____ ❖ _____

❖ _____ ❖ _____

❖ _____ ❖ _____

❖ _____ ❖ _____

❖ _____ ❖ _____

❖ _____ ❖ _____

❖ _____ ❖ _____

Directions:

_____

_____

_____

Category:
❑ Appetizer
❑ Beverage
❑ Sauce
❑ Soup
❑ Entrée
❑ Dessert

Type:
❑ Fish
❑ Meat
❑ Poultry
❑ Vegetables
❑ N/A

Prep Time:

Cook Time:

Servings:

_____

_____

_____

_____

_____

_____

Rating: ☆ ☆ ☆ ☆ ☆

Notes & Comments:

Recipe:

Ingredients:

- ❖
- ❖
- ❖
- ❖
- ❖
- ❖
- ❖

- ❖
- ❖
- ❖
- ❖
- ❖
- ❖
- ❖

Category:
- ❑ Appetizer
- ❑ Beverage
- ❑ Sauce
- ❑ Soup
- ❑ Entrée
- ❑ Dessert

Type:
- ❑ Fish
- ❑ Meat
- ❑ Poultry
- ❑ Vegetables
- ❑ N/A

Prep Time:

Cook Time:

Directions:

Servings:

Notes & Comments:

Recipe:

Ingredients:

❖ _____

❖ _____

❖ _____

❖ _____

❖ _____

❖ _____

❖ _____

❖ _____

❖ _____

❖ _____

❖ _____

❖ _____

❖ _____

❖ _____

Category:
❑ Appetizer
❑ Beverage
❑ Sauce
❑ Soup
❑ Entrée
❑ Dessert

Type:
❑ Fish
❑ Meat
❑ Poultry
❑ Vegetables
❑ N/A

Prep Time:

Cook Time:

Servings:

Directions:

Notes & Comments:

Recipe:

Ingredients:

- ❖
- ❖
- ❖
- ❖
- ❖
- ❖
- ❖

- ❖
- ❖
- ❖
- ❖
- ❖
- ❖
- ❖

Category:
- ☐ Appetizer
- ☐ Beverage
- ☐ Sauce
- ☐ Soup
- ☐ Entrée
- ☐ Dessert

Type:
- ☐ Fish
- ☐ Meat
- ☐ Poultry
- ☐ Vegetables
- ☐ N/A

Prep Time:

Cook Time:

Servings:

Directions:

Rating: ☆ ☆ ☆ ☆ ☆

Notes & Comments:

Recipe:

Ingredients:

❖ _____
❖ _____

❖ _____
❖ _____

❖ _____
❖ _____

❖ _____
❖ _____

❖ _____
❖ _____

❖ _____
❖ _____

❖ _____
❖ _____

Category:
❑ Appetizer
❑ Beverage
❑ Sauce
❑ Soup
❑ Entrée
❑ Dessert

Type:
❑ Fish
❑ Meat
❑ Poultry
❑ Vegetables
❑ N/A

Prep Time:

Cook Time:

Servings:

Directions:

_____

_____

_____

_____

_____

_____

_____

_____

_____

_____

Notes & Comments:

Recipe:

Ingredients:

- ❖
- ❖
- ❖
- ❖
- ❖
- ❖
- ❖

- ❖
- ❖
- ❖
- ❖
- ❖
- ❖
- ❖

Category:
- ☐ Appetizer
- ☐ Beverage
- ☐ Sauce
- ☐ Soup
- ☐ Entrée
- ☐ Dessert

Type:
- ☐ Fish
- ☐ Meat
- ☐ Poultry
- ☐ Vegetables
- ☐ N/A

Prep Time:

Cook Time:

Servings:

Directions:

Rating: ☆ ☆ ☆ ☆ ☆

Notes & Comments:

Recipe:

Ingredients:

- ❖ _____
- ❖ _____
- ❖ _____
- ❖ _____
- ❖ _____
- ❖ _____
- ❖ _____

- ❖ _____
- ❖ _____
- ❖ _____
- ❖ _____
- ❖ _____
- ❖ _____
- ❖ _____

Category:
- ❑ Appetizer
- ❑ Beverage
- ❑ Sauce
- ❑ Soup
- ❑ Entrée
- ❑ Dessert

Type:
- ❑ Fish
- ❑ Meat
- ❑ Poultry
- ❑ Vegetables
- ❑ N/A

Prep Time:

Cook Time:

Servings:

Directions:

_____

_____

_____

_____

_____

_____

_____

_____

_____

Rating: ☆ ☆ ☆ ☆ ☆

Notes & Comments:

Recipe:

Ingredients:

* ❖
* ❖
* ❖
* ❖
* ❖
* ❖
* ❖

* ❖
* ❖
* ❖
* ❖
* ❖
* ❖
* ❖

Category:
❑ Appetizer
❑ Beverage
❑ Sauce
❑ Soup
❑ Entrée
❑ Dessert

Type:
❑ Fish
❑ Meat
❑ Poultry
❑ Vegetables
❑ N/A

Prep Time:

Cook Time:

Servings:

Directions:

Rating: ☆ ☆ ☆ ☆ ☆

Notes & Comments:

Recipe:

Ingredients:

❖ _____

❖ _____

❖ _____

❖ _____

❖ _____

❖ _____

❖ _____

❖ _____

❖ _____

❖ _____

❖ _____

❖ _____

❖ _____

❖ _____

Category:
❑ Appetizer
❑ Beverage
❑ Sauce
❑ Soup
❑ Entrée
❑ Dessert

Type:
❑ Fish
❑ Meat
❑ Poultry
❑ Vegetables
❑ N/A

Prep Time:

Cook Time:

Servings:

Directions:

_____

_____

_____

_____

_____

_____

_____

_____

_____

Rating: ☆ ☆ ☆ ☆ ☆

Notes & Comments:

Recipe:

Ingredients:

❖ _____

❖ _____

❖ _____

❖ _____

❖ _____

❖ _____

❖ _____

❖ _____

❖ _____

❖ _____

❖ _____

❖ _____

❖ _____

❖ _____

Category:
❑ Appetizer
❑ Beverage
❑ Sauce
❑ Soup
❑ Entrée
❑ Dessert

Type:
❑ Fish
❑ Meat
❑ Poultry
❑ Vegetables
❑ N/A

Prep Time:

Cook Time:

Servings:

Directions:

_____

_____

_____

_____

_____

_____

_____

_____

_____

_____

_____

Rating: ☆ ☆ ☆ ☆ ☆

Notes & Comments:

Recipe:

Ingredients:

- ❖ _____
- ❖ _____
- ❖ _____
- ❖ _____
- ❖ _____
- ❖ _____
- ❖ _____

- ❖ _____
- ❖ _____
- ❖ _____
- ❖ _____
- ❖ _____
- ❖ _____
- ❖ _____

Category:
- ❑ Appetizer
- ❑ Beverage
- ❑ Sauce
- ❑ Soup
- ❑ Entrée
- ❑ Dessert

Type:
- ❑ Fish
- ❑ Meat
- ❑ Poultry
- ❑ Vegetables
- ❑ N/A

Prep Time:

Cook Time:

Servings:

Directions:

_____

_____

_____

_____

_____

_____

_____

_____

_____

_____

Rating: ☆ ☆ ☆ ☆ ☆

Notes & Comments:

Recipe:

Ingredients:

- ❖ _____
- ❖ _____
- ❖ _____
- ❖ _____
- ❖ _____
- ❖ _____
- ❖ _____

- ❖ _____
- ❖ _____
- ❖ _____
- ❖ _____
- ❖ _____
- ❖ _____
- ❖ _____

Category:
- ❑ Appetizer
- ❑ Beverage
- ❑ Sauce
- ❑ Soup
- ❑ Entrée
- ❑ Dessert

Type:
- ❑ Fish
- ❑ Meat
- ❑ Poultry
- ❑ Vegetables
- ❑ N/A

Prep Time:

Cook Time:

Servings:

Directions:

_____

_____

_____

_____

_____

_____

_____

_____

Rating: ☆ ☆ ☆ ☆ ☆

Notes & Comments:

Recipe:

Ingredients:

- ❖
- ❖
- ❖
- ❖
- ❖
- ❖
- ❖
- ❖
- ❖
- ❖
- ❖
- ❖
- ❖
- ❖

Directions:

Category:
- ❑ Appetizer
- ❑ Beverage
- ❑ Sauce
- ❑ Soup
- ❑ Entrée
- ❑ Dessert

Type:
- ❑ Fish
- ❑ Meat
- ❑ Poultry
- ❑ Vegetables
- ❑ N/A

Prep Time:

Cook Time:

Servings:

Rating: ☆ ☆ ☆ ☆ ☆

Notes & Comments:

Recipe:

Ingredients:

❖

❖

❖

❖

❖

❖

❖

❖

❖

❖

❖

❖

❖

❖

Directions:

Category:
❑ Appetizer
❑ Beverage
❑ Sauce
❑ Soup
❑ Entrée
❑ Dessert

Type:
❑ Fish
❑ Meat
❑ Poultry
❑ Vegetables
❑ N/A

Prep Time:

Cook Time:

Servings:

Rating: ☆ ☆ ☆ ☆ ☆

Notes & Comments:

Recipe:

Ingredients:

- ❖
- ❖
- ❖
- ❖
- ❖
- ❖
- ❖

- ❖
- ❖
- ❖
- ❖
- ❖
- ❖
- ❖

Category:
- ❑ Appetizer
- ❑ Beverage
- ❑ Sauce
- ❑ Soup
- ❑ Entrée
- ❑ Dessert

Type:
- ❑ Fish
- ❑ Meat
- ❑ Poultry
- ❑ Vegetables
- ❑ N/A

Prep Time:

Cook Time:

Servings:

Directions:

Rating: ☆ ☆ ☆ ☆ ☆

Notes & Comments:

Recipe:

Ingredients:

❖
❖

❖
❖

❖
❖

❖
❖

❖
❖

❖
❖

❖
❖

Category:
❑ Appetizer
❑ Beverage
❑ Sauce
❑ Soup
❑ Entrée
❑ Dessert

Type:
❑ Fish
❑ Meat
❑ Poultry
❑ Vegetables
❑ N/A

Prep Time:

Cook Time:

Servings:

Directions:

Rating: ☆ ☆ ☆ ☆ ☆

Notes & Comments:

Recipe:

Ingredients:

- ❖ _____
- ❖ _____
- ❖ _____
- ❖ _____
- ❖ _____
- ❖ _____
- ❖ _____

- ❖ _____
- ❖ _____
- ❖ _____
- ❖ _____
- ❖ _____
- ❖ _____
- ❖ _____

Category:
- ❑ Appetizer
- ❑ Beverage
- ❑ Sauce
- ❑ Soup
- ❑ Entrée
- ❑ Dessert

Type:
- ❑ Fish
- ❑ Meat
- ❑ Poultry
- ❑ Vegetables
- ❑ N/A

Prep Time:

Cook Time:

Servings:

Directions:

_____

_____

_____

_____

_____

_____

_____

_____

_____

Rating: ☆ ☆ ☆ ☆ ☆

Notes & Comments:

Recipe:

Ingredients:

❖ _____

❖ _____

❖ _____

❖ _____

❖ _____

❖ _____

❖ _____

❖ _____

❖ _____

❖ _____

❖ _____

❖ _____

❖ _____

❖ _____

Category:
❏ Appetizer
❏ Beverage
❏ Sauce
❏ Soup
❏ Entrée
❏ Dessert

Type:
❏ Fish
❏ Meat
❏ Poultry
❏ Vegetables
❏ N/A

Prep Time:

Cook Time:

Directions:

Servings:

_____

_____

_____

_____

_____

_____

_____

_____

Rating: ☆ ☆ ☆ ☆ ☆

Notes & Comments:

Recipe:

Ingredients:

❖ _____

❖ _____

❖ _____

❖ _____

❖ _____

❖ _____

❖ _____

❖ _____

❖ _____

❖ _____

❖ _____

❖ _____

❖ _____

❖ _____

Category:
❑ Appetizer
❑ Beverage
❑ Sauce
❑ Soup
❑ Entrée
❑ Dessert

Type:
❑ Fish
❑ Meat
❑ Poultry
❑ Vegetables
❑ N/A

Prep Time:

Cook Time:

Servings:

Directions:

_____

_____

_____

_____

_____

_____

_____

_____

_____

_____

_____

Rating: ☆ ☆ ☆ ☆ ☆

Notes & Comments:

Recipe:

Ingredients:

- ❖ _____
- ❖ _____
- ❖ _____
- ❖ _____
- ❖ _____
- ❖ _____
- ❖ _____

- ❖ _____
- ❖ _____
- ❖ _____
- ❖ _____
- ❖ _____
- ❖ _____
- ❖ _____

Category:
- ❑ Appetizer
- ❑ Beverage
- ❑ Sauce
- ❑ Soup
- ❑ Entrée
- ❑ Dessert

Type:
- ❑ Fish
- ❑ Meat
- ❑ Poultry
- ❑ Vegetables
- ❑ N/A

Prep Time:

Cook Time:

Servings:

Directions:

_____

_____

_____

_____

_____

_____

_____

_____

_____

_____

Rating: ☆ ☆ ☆ ☆ ☆

Notes & Comments:

Recipe:

Ingredients:

- ❖ _____
- ❖ _____
- ❖ _____
- ❖ _____
- ❖ _____
- ❖ _____
- ❖ _____

- ❖ _____
- ❖ _____
- ❖ _____
- ❖ _____
- ❖ _____
- ❖ _____
- ❖ _____

Category:
- ☐ Appetizer
- ☐ Beverage
- ☐ Sauce
- ☐ Soup
- ☐ Entrée
- ☐ Dessert

Type:
- ☐ Fish
- ☐ Meat
- ☐ Poultry
- ☐ Vegetables
- ☐ N/A

Prep Time:

Cook Time:

Servings:

Directions:

_____

_____

_____

_____

_____

_____

_____

_____

_____

Rating: ☆ ☆ ☆ ☆ ☆

Notes & Comments:

Recipe:

Ingredients:

❖ _____

❖ _____

❖ _____

❖ _____

❖ _____

❖ _____

❖ _____

❖ _____

❖ _____

❖ _____

❖ _____

❖ _____

❖ _____

❖ _____

Category:
☐ Appetizer
☐ Beverage
☐ Sauce
☐ Soup
☐ Entrée
☐ Dessert

Type:
☐ Fish
☐ Meat
☐ Poultry
☐ Vegetables
☐ N/A

Prep Time:

Cook Time:

Servings:

Directions:

_____

_____

_____

_____

_____

_____

_____

_____

_____

_____

_____

Rating: ☆ ☆ ☆ ☆ ☆

Notes & Comments:

Recipe:

Ingredients:

- ❖
- ❖
- ❖
- ❖
- ❖
- ❖
- ❖

- ❖
- ❖
- ❖
- ❖
- ❖
- ❖
- ❖

Category:
- ❑ Appetizer
- ❑ Beverage
- ❑ Sauce
- ❑ Soup
- ❑ Entrée
- ❑ Dessert

Type:
- ❑ Fish
- ❑ Meat
- ❑ Poultry
- ❑ Vegetables
- ❑ N/A

Prep Time:

Cook Time:

Servings:

Directions:

Rating: ☆ ☆ ☆ ☆ ☆

Notes & Comments:

Recipe:

Ingredients:

- ❖ _____
- ❖ _____
- ❖ _____
- ❖ _____
- ❖ _____
- ❖ _____
- ❖ _____

- ❖ _____
- ❖ _____
- ❖ _____
- ❖ _____
- ❖ _____
- ❖ _____
- ❖ _____

Category:
- ❑ Appetizer
- ❑ Beverage
- ❑ Sauce
- ❑ Soup
- ❑ Entrée
- ❑ Dessert

Type:
- ❑ Fish
- ❑ Meat
- ❑ Poultry
- ❑ Vegetables
- ❑ N/A

Prep Time:

Cook Time:

Servings:

Directions:

_____

_____

_____

_____

_____

_____

_____

_____

Rating: ☆ ☆ ☆ ☆ ☆

Notes & Comments:

Recipe:

Ingredients:

- ❖ _____
- ❖ _____
- ❖ _____
- ❖ _____
- ❖ _____
- ❖ _____
- ❖ _____

- ❖ _____
- ❖ _____
- ❖ _____
- ❖ _____
- ❖ _____
- ❖ _____
- ❖ _____

Category:
- ❑ Appetizer
- ❑ Beverage
- ❑ Sauce
- ❑ Soup
- ❑ Entrée
- ❑ Dessert

Type:
- ❑ Fish
- ❑ Meat
- ❑ Poultry
- ❑ Vegetables
- ❑ N/A

Prep Time:

Cook Time:

Servings:

Directions:

_____

_____

_____

_____

_____

_____

_____

_____

_____

_____

Rating: ☆ ☆ ☆ ☆ ☆

Notes & Comments:

Recipe:

Ingredients:

❖ _____
❖ _____
❖ _____
❖ _____
❖ _____
❖ _____
❖ _____

❖ _____
❖ _____
❖ _____
❖ _____
❖ _____
❖ _____
❖ _____

Category:
❑ Appetizer
❑ Beverage
❑ Sauce
❑ Soup
❑ Entrée
❑ Dessert

Type:
❑ Fish
❑ Meat
❑ Poultry
❑ Vegetables
❑ N/A

Prep Time:

Cook Time:

Servings:

Directions:

Rating: ☆ ☆ ☆ ☆ ☆

Notes & Comments:

Recipe:

Ingredients:

- ❖
- ❖
- ❖
- ❖
- ❖
- ❖
- ❖

- ❖
- ❖
- ❖
- ❖
- ❖
- ❖
- ❖

Category:
- ❑ Appetizer
- ❑ Beverage
- ❑ Sauce
- ❑ Soup
- ❑ Entrée
- ❑ Dessert

Type:
- ❑ Fish
- ❑ Meat
- ❑ Poultry
- ❑ Vegetables
- ❑ N/A

Prep Time:

Cook Time:

Servings:

Directions:

Rating: ☆ ☆ ☆ ☆ ☆

61

Notes & Comments:

Recipe:

Ingredients:

- ❖
- ❖
- ❖
- ❖
- ❖
- ❖
- ❖

- ❖
- ❖
- ❖
- ❖
- ❖
- ❖
- ❖

Category:
- ❏ Appetizer
- ❏ Beverage
- ❏ Sauce
- ❏ Soup
- ❏ Entrée
- ❏ Dessert

Type:
- ❏ Fish
- ❏ Meat
- ❏ Poultry
- ❏ Vegetables
- ❏ N/A

Prep Time:

Cook Time:

Servings:

Directions:

Rating: ☆ ☆ ☆ ☆ ☆

Notes & Comments:

Recipe:

Ingredients:

❖
❖
❖
❖
❖
❖
❖

❖
❖
❖
❖
❖
❖
❖

Category:
❑ Appetizer
❑ Beverage
❑ Sauce
❑ Soup
❑ Entrée
❑ Dessert

Type:
❑ Fish
❑ Meat
❑ Poultry
❑ Vegetables
❑ N/A

Prep Time:

Cook Time:

Servings:

Directions:

Notes & Comments:

Recipe:

Ingredients:

❖

❖

❖

❖

❖

❖

❖

❖

❖

❖

❖

❖

❖

❖

Category:
❑ Appetizer
❑ Beverage
❑ Sauce
❑ Soup
❑ Entrée
❑ Dessert

Type:
❑ Fish
❑ Meat
❑ Poultry
❑ Vegetables
❑ N/A

Prep Time:

Cook Time:

Servings:

Directions:

Rating: ☆ ☆ ☆ ☆ ☆

Notes & Comments:

Recipe:

Ingredients:

❖

❖

❖

❖

❖

❖

❖

❖

❖

❖

❖

❖

❖

❖

Directions:

Category:
❑ Appetizer
❑ Beverage
❑ Sauce
❑ Soup
❑ Entrée
❑ Dessert

Type:
❑ Fish
❑ Meat
❑ Poultry
❑ Vegetables
❑ N/A

Prep Time:

Cook Time:

Servings:

Rating: ☆ ☆ ☆ ☆ ☆

Notes & Comments:

Recipe:

Ingredients:

❖ _____   ❖ _____

❖ _____   ❖ _____

❖ _____   ❖ _____

❖ _____   ❖ _____

❖ _____   ❖ _____

❖ _____   ❖ _____

❖ _____   ❖ _____

Directions:

_____

_____

_____

_____

_____

_____

_____

_____

_____

_____

Category:
❑ Appetizer
❑ Beverage
❑ Sauce
❑ Soup
❑ Entrée
❑ Dessert

Type:
❑ Fish
❑ Meat
❑ Poultry
❑ Vegetables
❑ N/A

Prep Time:

Cook Time:

Servings:

Rating: ☆ ☆ ☆ ☆ ☆

Notes & Comments:

Recipe:

Ingredients:

❖ _____
❖ _____
❖ _____
❖ _____
❖ _____
❖ _____
❖ _____

❖ _____
❖ _____
❖ _____
❖ _____
❖ _____
❖ _____
❖ _____

Category:
❑ Appetizer
❑ Beverage
❑ Sauce
❑ Soup
❑ Entrée
❑ Dessert

Type:
❑ Fish
❑ Meat
❑ Poultry
❑ Vegetables
❑ N/A

Prep Time:

Cook Time:

Servings:

Directions:

_____

_____

_____

_____

_____

_____

_____

_____

_____

_____

Rating: ☆ ☆ ☆ ☆ ☆

Notes & Comments:

Recipe:

Ingredients:

- ❖ _____
- ❖ _____
- ❖ _____
- ❖ _____
- ❖ _____
- ❖ _____
- ❖ _____

- ❖ _____
- ❖ _____
- ❖ _____
- ❖ _____
- ❖ _____
- ❖ _____
- ❖ _____

Category:
- ❑ Appetizer
- ❑ Beverage
- ❑ Sauce
- ❑ Soup
- ❑ Entrée
- ❑ Dessert

Type:
- ❑ Fish
- ❑ Meat
- ❑ Poultry
- ❑ Vegetables
- ❑ N/A

Prep Time:

Cook Time:

Directions:

Servings:

Notes & Comments:

Recipe:

Ingredients:

- ❖ _____
- ❖ _____
- ❖ _____
- ❖ _____
- ❖ _____
- ❖ _____
- ❖ _____

- ❖ _____
- ❖ _____
- ❖ _____
- ❖ _____
- ❖ _____
- ❖ _____
- ❖ _____

Category:
- ❑ Appetizer
- ❑ Beverage
- ❑ Sauce
- ❑ Soup
- ❑ Entrée
- ❑ Dessert

Type:
- ❑ Fish
- ❑ Meat
- ❑ Poultry
- ❑ Vegetables
- ❑ N/A

Prep Time:

Cook Time:

Directions:

Servings:

Notes & Comments:

Recipe:

Ingredients:

❖ _____
❖ _____

❖ _____
❖ _____

❖ _____
❖ _____

❖ _____
❖ _____

❖ _____
❖ _____

❖ _____
❖ _____

❖ _____
❖ _____

Category:
❏ Appetizer
❏ Beverage
❏ Sauce
❏ Soup
❏ Entrée
❏ Dessert

Type:
❏ Fish
❏ Meat
❏ Poultry
❏ Vegetables
❏ N/A

Prep Time:

Cook Time:

Servings:

Directions:

_____
_____
_____

_____
_____
_____
_____
_____
_____
_____

Rating: ☆ ☆ ☆ ☆ ☆

Notes & Comments:

Recipe:

Ingredients:

❖ _____
❖ _____
❖ _____
❖ _____
❖ _____
❖ _____
❖ _____

❖ _____
❖ _____
❖ _____
❖ _____
❖ _____
❖ _____
❖ _____

Category:
❑ Appetizer
❑ Beverage
❑ Sauce
❑ Soup
❑ Entrée
❑ Dessert

Type:
❑ Fish
❑ Meat
❑ Poultry
❑ Vegetables
❑ N/A

Prep Time:

Cook Time:

Servings:

Directions:

Notes & Comments:

Recipe:

Ingredients:

- ❖
- ❖
- ❖
- ❖
- ❖
- ❖
- ❖

- ❖
- ❖
- ❖
- ❖
- ❖
- ❖
- ❖

Category:
- ❑ Appetizer
- ❑ Beverage
- ❑ Sauce
- ❑ Soup
- ❑ Entrée
- ❑ Dessert

Type:
- ❑ Fish
- ❑ Meat
- ❑ Poultry
- ❑ Vegetables
- ❑ N/A

Prep Time:

Cook Time:

Servings:

Directions:

Rating: ☆ ☆ ☆ ☆ ☆

Notes & Comments:

Recipe:

Ingredients:

- ❖
- ❖
- ❖
- ❖
- ❖
- ❖
- ❖

- ❖
- ❖
- ❖
- ❖
- ❖
- ❖
- ❖

Category:
- ❑ Appetizer
- ❑ Beverage
- ❑ Sauce
- ❑ Soup
- ❑ Entrée
- ❑ Dessert

Type:
- ❑ Fish
- ❑ Meat
- ❑ Poultry
- ❑ Vegetables
- ❑ N/A

Prep Time:

Cook Time:

Servings:

Directions:

Rating: ☆ ☆ ☆ ☆ ☆

Notes & Comments:

Recipe:

Ingredients:

- ❖ _____
- ❖ _____
- ❖ _____
- ❖ _____
- ❖ _____
- ❖ _____
- ❖ _____

- ❖ _____
- ❖ _____
- ❖ _____
- ❖ _____
- ❖ _____
- ❖ _____
- ❖ _____

Category:
- ❑ Appetizer
- ❑ Beverage
- ❑ Sauce
- ❑ Soup
- ❑ Entrée
- ❑ Dessert

Type:
- ❑ Fish
- ❑ Meat
- ❑ Poultry
- ❑ Vegetables
- ❑ N/A

Prep Time:

Cook Time:

Servings:

Directions:

_____

_____

_____

_____

_____

_____

_____

_____

_____

Rating: ☆ ☆ ☆ ☆ ☆

Notes & Comments:

Recipe:

Ingredients:

- ❖ _____
- ❖ _____
- ❖ _____
- ❖ _____
- ❖ _____
- ❖ _____
- ❖ _____

- ❖ _____
- ❖ _____
- ❖ _____
- ❖ _____
- ❖ _____
- ❖ _____
- ❖ _____

Category:
- ❑ Appetizer
- ❑ Beverage
- ❑ Sauce
- ❑ Soup
- ❑ Entrée
- ❑ Dessert

Type:
- ❑ Fish
- ❑ Meat
- ❑ Poultry
- ❑ Vegetables
- ❑ N/A

Prep Time:

Cook Time:

Servings:

Directions:

_____

_____

_____

_____

_____

_____

_____

_____

_____

Rating: ☆ ☆ ☆ ☆ ☆

Notes & Comments:

Recipe:

Ingredients:

❖

❖

❖

❖

❖

❖

❖

❖

❖

❖

❖

❖

❖

❖

Directions:

Category:
☐ Appetizer
☐ Beverage
☐ Sauce
☐ Soup
☐ Entrée
☐ Dessert

Type:
☐ Fish
☐ Meat
☐ Poultry
☐ Vegetables
☐ N/A

Prep Time:

Cook Time:

Servings:

Rating: ☆ ☆ ☆ ☆ ☆

Notes & Comments:

Recipe:

Ingredients:

❖ _____
❖ _____
❖ _____
❖ _____
❖ _____
❖ _____
❖ _____

❖ _____
❖ _____
❖ _____
❖ _____
❖ _____
❖ _____
❖ _____

Category:
❑ Appetizer
❑ Beverage
❑ Sauce
❑ Soup
❑ Entrée
❑ Dessert

Type:
❑ Fish
❑ Meat
❑ Poultry
❑ Vegetables
❑ N/A

Prep Time:

Cook Time:

Servings:

Directions:

_____

Rating: ☆ ☆ ☆ ☆ ☆

Notes & Comments:

Recipe:

Ingredients:

❖ _____

❖ _____

❖ _____

❖ _____

❖ _____

❖ _____

❖ _____

❖ _____

❖ _____

❖ _____

❖ _____

❖ _____

❖ _____

❖ _____

Directions:

Category:
❑ Appetizer
❑ Beverage
❑ Sauce
❑ Soup
❑ Entrée
❑ Dessert

Type:
❑ Fish
❑ Meat
❑ Poultry
❑ Vegetables
❑ N/A

Prep Time:

Cook Time:

Servings:

Notes & Comments:

Recipe:

Ingredients:

- ❖ _____
- ❖ _____
- ❖ _____
- ❖ _____
- ❖ _____
- ❖ _____
- ❖ _____

- ❖ _____
- ❖ _____
- ❖ _____
- ❖ _____
- ❖ _____
- ❖ _____
- ❖ _____

Category:
- ❑ Appetizer
- ❑ Beverage
- ❑ Sauce
- ❑ Soup
- ❑ Entrée
- ❑ Dessert

Type:
- ❑ Fish
- ❑ Meat
- ❑ Poultry
- ❑ Vegetables
- ❑ N/A

Prep Time:

Cook Time:

Servings:

Directions:

_____

_____

_____

_____

_____

_____

_____

_____

_____

Rating: ☆ ☆ ☆ ☆ ☆

Notes & Comments:

Recipe:

Ingredients:

- ❖
- ❖
- ❖
- ❖
- ❖
- ❖
- ❖

- ❖
- ❖
- ❖
- ❖
- ❖
- ❖
- ❖

Category:
- ☐ Appetizer
- ☐ Beverage
- ☐ Sauce
- ☐ Soup
- ☐ Entrée
- ☐ Dessert

Type:
- ☐ Fish
- ☐ Meat
- ☐ Poultry
- ☐ Vegetables
- ☐ N/A

Prep Time:

Cook Time:

Servings:

Directions:

Rating: ☆ ☆ ☆ ☆ ☆

Notes & Comments:

Recipe:

Ingredients:

- ❖
- ❖
- ❖
- ❖
- ❖
- ❖
- ❖

- ❖
- ❖
- ❖
- ❖
- ❖
- ❖
- ❖

Category:
- ❏ Appetizer
- ❏ Beverage
- ❏ Sauce
- ❏ Soup
- ❏ Entrée
- ❏ Dessert

Type:
- ❏ Fish
- ❏ Meat
- ❏ Poultry
- ❏ Vegetables
- ❏ N/A

Prep Time:

Directions:

Cook Time:

Servings:

Rating: ☆ ☆ ☆ ☆ ☆

Notes & Comments:

For more amazing journals and adult colouring books from Penelope Pewter, visit:

Amazon.com
CreateSpace.com
RWSquaredMedia.Wordpress.com

She Believed She Could
So She Did Adult Coloring Book

The Be A Pineapple
Adult Coloring Book

The Matryoshka Nesting Doll
Coloring Book for Adults

The Adult Coloring Book
for Coffee Lovers

Made in the USA
San Bernardino, CA
20 November 2018